Choosing to See the Hand of God

Teresa A. Bolden

Choosing to See the Hand of God
ISBN: Softcover 978-1-951472-71-9
Copyright © 2020 by Teresa A. Bolden

All rights reserved. No part of this book may be reproduced or transmitted in any form or by any means, electronic or mechanical, including photocopying, recording, or by any information storage and retrieval system, without permission in writing from the publisher.

www.parsonsporch.com

Choosing to See the Hand of God

It gives me great joy to dedicate this book to my precious jewels:

Joyce, Nathanael (Theo), and Kristine Bolden. These words are scripted right from my heart. It is my hope that each of you learn to embrace your faith in our trustworthy Father, especially in the tough times. I am delighted that GOD has allowed me to be your mother, teacher, mentor, and friend. The most important lesson that I would have you to learn is to
FIX YOUR FOCUS ON JESUS!

In honor to GOD & in memory of Nathaniel T. Bolden, Sr.

With all my
"TeeWee"

Table of Contents

Choosing to See the Hand of God 9

In the Preparations 14

In His Provisions 19

In the Unknown 22

In the Midst of my Shaken Foundation 26

In the Surrender 30

In Secondary Losses 33

In My Grief 37

In Moments of Mourning 40

In My Praise 43

In HIS Promises 46

In HIS Perfect Timing 50

Choosing to See the Hand of God

May 25th, 2019 was the first day of my new life without my husband. I had been married to Nathaniel longer than I had been single. We married when I was 19 years old and we were looking forward to celebrating our 27th anniversary that upcoming July. However, Nathaniel was diagnosed with a brain tumor on April 5th, 2019 and was scheduled to have surgery on May 9th. It seemed to have happened all too quickly: Unfortunately, the surgery did not go as we had hoped and prayed, or according to the surgeon's "best case scenario."

The two weeks between the surgery date and the day Nathaniel went to be with the Lord were the most emotionally draining days of our lives. Thankfully, our adult children, Joyce, Theo, and Kristine, made sure that I was never alone at the hospital or hotel. Joyce, our oldest, ran interference for phone calls or any other necessary business. Our churches, friends, and families encouraged us through their prayers and by providing snacks and money.

Nathaniel's specific request was to have no outside visitors while in the hospital: although it was extremely difficult, we complied. Instead, several friends came to the hospital just to sit with me downstairs in the waiting area. Text messages were a tangible reminder of just how enveloped we were in love and prayers. They were our strength and fortitude during such a traumatic time of uncertainty.

In the immediate days after Nathaniel's death, we had so much love poured on us through visits, prayers, food, snacks, and financial support. Admittedly, I was just walking around on autopilot, still in shock. There were so many special people who dropped by with prayers, hugs, and concerns. Too many to name. I am glad for most of the visits, but some people haven't learned the art of just being with another in their pain; not always having to say something to fill the silence, not giving clichés of how the loved one is in a better place now, and not giving opinions of how the bereaved should feel, act, or respond.

In times past, I am sure that I've been guilty of awkward, inappropriate responses during someone's tragedy or loss. The loss of my husband reminded me that death is always uncomfortable since we were created to live forever. There are no words to soothe the ache or to change what has happened. No one is expected to make it all better for the grieving. Sometimes it is best to just sit, minister to their needs as prompted, and use meaningful words when necessary. I am extremely grateful to everyone who did just that!

Pastor Andrew Betts and his beautiful wife, Sarah, visited my family as we were grieving Nathaniel's death. Andrew was Kristine's previous youth pastor when she was in high school. After Kristine graduated, she and Joyce were able to minister with him through the youth programs at Crossroad Community Church. As Andrew and Sarah sat with us the day after the passing of my husband, they both gave their condolences, and then we had casual conversation.

Out of nowhere, Andrew asked, "So, tell me where each of you have seen the hand of God during this ordeal?" I'm not even sure that he knew just how he was being used by God.

What an odd question, one might say, especially at a time like this. However, even in the midst of my shock, I immediately knew that this was a profound question that would propel my family to shift our focus. As Christians, we grieve with hope and are instructed to *give thanks in everything* (1 Thessalonians 5:18). We don't have to be thankful *for* everything, but in everything.

Many times, in adverse situations, it can seem impossible to see beyond the horrendous circumstance that's right in front of us. Despite my heavy grief, I had already witnessed the hand of God. Pastor Andrew's question would now challenge me to make a conscious choice to see God amid all the pain.

Throughout my life, I have often found journaling to be emotionally therapeutic and spiritually refreshing. It did not surprise me when I turned to paper and pen for release and solace. I was able to put some of my emotions into words despite the tears that welled up and dropped onto the papers.

The following pages are excerpts of personal thoughts, feelings, and experiences during my earliest days of navigating my grief. As you read along, my sincerest prayer is that you will be encouraged to choose to see the hand of our loving Father in each of life's challenges. During your darkest times, may you be reminded that His plans are always good. *In this world, we will have trouble, but He has overcome the world* (John

16:33). If you know the Overcomer, you can take courage!

If you struggle to see the hand of God in your toughest times, that's quite alright, too. Just make the personal decision to give Him your sacrificial praise, your steadfast trust, *and* your broken heart. God will always show up.

Insight

1) Have you or are you currently facing an incredible circumstance?

2) Have you viewed God as close or distant during your difficult time(s)?

3) Write a prayer about your experiences and feelings. Be honest by telling God exactly what is in your heart.

_____
_____
_____
_____
_____
_____
_____
_____
_____
_____
_____
_____
_____
_____
_____
_____

Point to Ponder:

The Lord your God in your midst, The Mighty One, will save… Zeph. 3:17 NKJV

In the Preparations

The first thing that I am mindful of is the fact that nothing takes God by surprise. For me, the visit to the neurosurgeon on a late Friday afternoon had my stomach in knots. I was bewildered by the diagnosis and the thought of brain surgery. Our ride back home was almost in complete silence. I was nervous and uneasy about a pending surgery. Even though Nathaniel did not say much, I could tell that his thoughts were racing. When he did speak, he expressed his wishes for how to handle the hospital stay and visitors. He also had his own way and timing of who he wanted to tell: I respected his desires and left it up to him who he would tell and when.

We knew that we wanted to tell our children about the upcoming surgery. However, Joyce was away at a church event, and Theo lived close to three hours away. Kristine, our youngest daughter, was the only one that was at home after the first doctor's visit. We also had a family gathering scheduled at our house for the following day. It was my dad's birthday celebration, so I tried to set the news aside in order to get through the day.

The next day, Saturday, I went to the grocery store in preparation for Dad's birthday celebration. There, I ran into my brother's pastor, Vanessa Lee Stephens. As God would have it, I told her about the upcoming surgery. I'm not even sure how the words came out, since I hadn't yet mentally processed this information. After listening to me, she said that she would send me a book of prayers for healing, and she did. That was the beginning of an ongoing prayer connection with her that God orchestrated for the days, weeks, and months ahead. Yes, the hand of God!

During prayer time at church on Sunday morning, I felt prompted to go to my pastor's wife, Debbie Kiser. I didn't move right away, struggling with whether I wanted to say anything for two reasons: 1) we hadn't told our children yet, and 2) saying the words aloud would make it more real. However, by the end of the second song, the urge to seek out Debbie was stronger. I walked toward the back of the church, and up the other side toward where she was standing. She immediately turned to me, and I asked if she would go to the altar with me. She replied with excitement, "God told me that I'd be praying with you today! I wasn't sure if I was supposed to go to you…"

At the altar, I explained our dilemma and stressed the point that our children had not yet been told. Debbie prayed specific prayers for us for healing, peace, direction, wisdom, and especially for the doctors. Lastly, she asked God to give me a "word" *today*.

Later that afternoon, while cleaning, crying, and praying, I received my word from the Lord:

When you don't know, let it lead you to what you do know.

That's it. I repeated the phrase at least three times, and with tears streaming down my face, I began to tell God, "I don't know what we are facing here. I don't know if this is cancer. I don't know if Nathaniel will be blind, lame, or otherwise impaired. But, God, I know that

You are faithful. You are the Great Physician. You are in control and You are with me…"

I cannot remember all that I said but I do remember that I experienced the overwhelming presence of the Lord. I began to think about one of the worst times in my life; the death of my mother when I was just 17 years old. I felt like GOD was reminding me that He was with me then, now, and forever will be. When I thought that I could not survive losing Mom, GOD sustained me.

That night after I prayed with Debbie, Nathaniel and I told each of our children exactly what we knew. We have always communicated openly and our family has leaned into the power of prayer. We decided to join our hearts in prayer for this situation as well.

On Sunday morning, April 28th, I was headed to church by myself. Although I did not hear an audible voice, I recognized the spirit of the Lord telling me to "prepare for change." I was so moved by what I sensed that I pulled over to the side of the road. I texted Theo, asking him to call me when he got a chance and I explained that it was not an emergency. To my surprise, Theo returned the call swiftly. He said that he was in between services at his own church in Maryland.

I told him what I had just experienced and asked him to be in prayer for me throughout the upcoming week. I explained that I was unsure if the preparation was for permanent or temporary change. However, he knew that I had been struggling with Nathaniel's decision to move forward with the surgery. I needed God to fix my heart so that if the surgery did leave Nathaniel impaired, I would not have a resentful or an "I told you so" kind of attitude. I wanted to be able to minister to my husband, their dad, with a clear, clean, heart.

How humbled I was to hear Theo pray for me unlike I had heard before. His insight and maturity was apparent as he prayed the words that touched my heart and expressed my sentiment. I remember hearing him ask God to give me His peace and to strengthen me to be whatever Nathaniel needed in the coming weeks. I thanked Theo and we exchanged "I love you's", as we both needed to get into our services. Sitting in my car in the church parking lot, I said, "Thank you Lord for the privilege of prayer."

Insight

"When you don't know, let it lead you to what you do know."

1) What are some undeniable truths that you know about GOD? From Scripture? From past personal experience?
2) List reasons that you can trust GOD.
3) Write a prayer to GOD listing any barriers that keep you from trusting Him. Be honest by telling God exactly what is in your heart.

_____
_____
_____
_____
_____
_____
_____
_____
_____
_____
_____
_____
_____
_____

Point to Ponder:

"... your Father knows the things you have need of before you ask Him." Matthew 6:8

In His Provisions

We had been told that we should expect Nathaniel to be hospitalized for about four days; two days in the Intensive Care Unit and two days on the regular floor. A few days before his surgery, I received a phone call from two very special people who had decided to give me a substantial donation to help with hotel stay, food, gas, or other needs. What an unexpected gift of love!

An anticipated four-day hospital stay turned into twelve days in the hospital the first time, two days home, and two days back in the hospital. I stayed the entire time, with exception of one night, while the children traveled back-and-forth. That meant there were tolls, food, gas, and lodging expenses. Not to mention the unexpected window replacement, due to a string of car burglaries at the hotel where we were staying. Who could've known that we would need the extra financial support that our friends and family had extended? *Who?* Our all-knowing God! Look at His hand of provision, supplying funds that I didn't even know that I *would be* needing. Thank you, Jesus!

One thing I have learned about choosing to see the hand of God is that it means shifting my perspective. In looking for things for which to be grateful, I find these:

1) Thank God that I had the means to get a nice hotel so that I could get a warm shower and rest my body, even if for short periods of time.

2) Thank God that only my window was broken and not Kristine's and Joyce's. That would have been three times the finances!
3) Thank God that it was just my window, not mindless vandalism.
4) Thank God for safety since the police report stated that a gun was stolen from one of the vehicles. That person could have easily walked into the hotel and started shooting.

I am so grateful that our God is never taken by surprise! God was never unaware or unprepared for the days ahead. *All the days ordained for me were written in your book before one of them came to be (Psalm 139: 16b).* Our days are in His hands!

Insight

1) Have you ever received an unexpected gift or act of kindness? How did you feel?

2) In what way(s) was the gift helpful to you?

3) Write a prayer to GOD about a time that you have seen something good that came out of a difficult situation. How could things have been worse? Be honest by telling God exactly what is in your heart.

_____
_____
_____
_____
_____
_____
_____
_____
_____
_____
_____
_____
_____
_____
_____

Point to Ponder:

Choosing to see the hand of GOD means shifting one's perspective.

In the Unknown

The events surrounding Nathaniel's surgery and hospitalization remain incomprehensible, even to this day. My heart cannot understand what my ears and eyes have observed. Nathaniel experienced over nine and a half hours of brain surgery, at least three strokes, large blood clots, vision impairment, and endocrine and adrenal complications. I will never know exactly what went wrong... I will never know why it had to end this way... I will never know why... there are so many unknowns!

This is the place where I struggled most to see the hand of God. I would fall asleep and wake up with questions. As tears stained my pillow, I'd pray, "Lord, I don't know what has happened... this hardly seems real. I am a widow after almost 27 years of marriage. My husband, friend, and life partner is gone. I walked into the hospital beside Nathaniel who was standing tall and full of life. Days later, I've watched him take his last breath, yet it is still unbelievable. I am in an emotional fog and physically exhausted."

I never knew that grief could be so tiresome. Although I was tired, I was not sleepy because my body and brain were moving at two different paces--- slow motion and turbo speed! Every time I would get still, my mind would race to discover another piece of business to be taken care of or one more phone call that needed to be made. My heart ached with each recounting of my husband's name, social security number, date of death, and removing him from all our business accounts and official documents: The reality of such finality. Nathaniel is gone, never to return. My heart just hurts.

During difficult times like these, I would rally everything within me to say, "I trust You, Lord." I couldn't see His hand, but I trusted His heart. The undeniable truth that I *knew* is that God loved me, and God is good!

So, where do I see the hand of God? I'm glad that you asked. Initially, I didn't understand or agree with Nathaniel's decision to prohibit visitors during his hospital stay. However, I believe that because of that decision we were gifted with such precious, intimate moments during Nathaniel's last days and hours on this side of eternity. In spite of his rapidly failing health, the doctors were astounded by Nathaniel's alertness and his mental ability to talk to each of us with clarity, determination, and purpose. In our uncertainty of each next moment, we still had times of laughter. This is one that I will share: in between labored breathing, Nathaniel looked at me and told me that I was "slacking on my job." He wanted me to keep his lips moistened with his lip balm. I said to him, "You still look good." He responded, "I'm supposed to look great."

That's our Nathaniel!

As Theo said at Nathaniel's memorial service on June 1st, "what a good feeling to know that we love God and each other, we've shared our hearts, and there are no regrets. We know that we will see him again."

The last scriptural reference that I heard Nathaniel say was *"to be absent from the body is to be present with the Lord"* (2 Corinthians 5:8). Thank You, Lord!

Insight

Are you struggling with unanswered questions, unknowns, and "whys?"

1) List them on a separate sheet of paper.
2) Take time to read over each one.
3) Ask yourself the following question:
   Even if I had all of these answers, would it change the present situation?
4) Write a prayer to GOD asking Him to help you to release every question, regret, and unknown. Give Him permission to fill your heart and mind with hope and trust in His love. Be honest by telling God exactly what is in your heart.

_____
_____
_____
_____
_____
_____
_____
_____
_____
_____
_____
_____
_____
_____

Point to Ponder:
Trust in the Lord with all thine heart; lean not to your own understanding. Proverbs 3:5

In the Midst of my Shaken Foundation

Nothing will ever be the same! Everything is different as I struggle to find my way through this fog. Being with friends and family is a constant reminder of the biggest void I have ever experienced. Conversations are different, jokes aren't as funny, and life is just not as full.

Following Nathaniel's death, I realized that I was both emotionally numb and paralyzed, unable to think about the next thing. How can I make short-term or long-term plans? What does the future hold for me? It was extremely difficult going through my calendar and having to cancel doctor appointments that had been scheduled for Nathaniel. Looking at the heart shaped symbol around our anniversary date left an incomparable heaviness. Who knew that Nathaniel would die just seven and a half weeks before our 27th wedding anniversary? All my plans have been shattered. How do I move forward? Where do I go from here?

Also, thoughts in my mind chanted, *"If I can lose my husband unexpectedly, then anything can happen."* One Sunday afternoon, I was in the house preparing for my family to come over. Joyce had backed into the driveway after church and I was waiting for her to enter the house. After a few minutes, I realized that she was still in her car in the driveway. When I looked outside, her head was down and her glasses appeared to be sliding off her face, as if she had fainted. I jolted out the door, realizing that her car was still running. My heart sank as I rushed toward the car.

She looked up at me, and I realized that she was just reading. She recognized the utter fear on my face, and I burst into tears. Even though I knew that she was okay, my emotions had already taken me on an exaggerated roller coaster ride.

In addition to everything else, on August 12th, three days after my yearly mammogram, I was scheduled for a follow-up visit because the doctor found an abnormality. They did a second mammogram and an ultrasound. Then, the radiologist came in to ask me which surgeon I had a preference to see. Eventually, I was scheduled for a consultation and a biopsy.

Suddenly, I was thrust back into the medical world of uncertainty, never doubting what God CAN do, but surely questioning what He would. This felt like another whirlwind. The biopsy was a new experience for me that bombarded my head and heart with traumatic triggers. I anxiously walked down hospital hallways, wondering what would be next. I am thankful for the doctor and the surgical technician who were extremely kind and gentle with me. There were times that I couldn't get my words to come out of my mouth—grief stricken and paralyzed. Sabrina, the technician just patiently waited until I could gather my thoughts and respond to basic questions. In addition, Dr. Carey was thorough with his explanation of every step in the biopsy procedure, which helped me to be less fearful.

It was during these emotional days between the mammogram call back and the biopsy appointment that I plunged into my writing. This helped me to recall the many ways that God has been with me thus far. *"Surely, He will not forsake me now."* That's what I had to say aloud to myself whenever I became overwhelmed by fear and "what-ifs." *When my heart is overwhelmed lead me to the rock that is higher than I* (Psalm 61:2). Yes, I have faith and I believe God is my Healer. However, my recent loss has reinforced the truth that God will always answer my prayers, but not necessarily the way I expect. Thus, the task is learning to trust His plan.

I received the awaited phone call and heard, "Teresa, there's no cancer cells. You're good."

Thank You, Lord!

I exhaled and cried tears of relief! Then I prayed, "Lord I thank You for this good news and for being with me once *again*. Could You please give me renewed joy, purpose, and passion? I'm emotionally worn but spiritually charged. Can I wake up with something good and positive upon which to direct my focus and energy? Lord, is there anything that *I* can do for You?"

There will always be unknowns, but *GOD has not given us a spirit of fear* (2 Timothy 1:7). I will continually learn to rest in God's *perfect love that casts out all fear* (1 John 4:18).

Insight

1)   List all of the ways that your loss, grief, and adversity has affected areas of your life.

_____
_____
_____
_____

2)   Write a prayer to GOD telling Him about every pain, fear, and feeling of unrest. Be honest by telling God exactly what is in your heart.

_____
_____
_____
_____
_____
_____
_____
_____
_____
_____
_____
_____
_____
_____

Point to Ponder:
The muscle that you exercise most is the one that becomes the strongest! Your choice--- fear or faith.

In the Surrender

Prior to my husband passing away, my dad had emergency brain surgery on December 8, 2018 and suffered a grand seizure in the recovery room. He was put on 100% life-support and we were told that his chances of survival were slim. When Dad eventually woke up, the doctors tried removing the breathing tube six different times. However, my father's lungs were not strong enough to breathe without the assistance of the machine. I remember looking at my father and thinking how strange it was seeing him communicate using only his eyes. It was unbearable to realize that the machine was doing all the breathing for him.

The morning that we were thinking we would have to make some major decisions about my dad, Nathaniel grabbed both my hands and prayed a short, but sincere prayer in our hotel room, "Lord, let this be a better day. In Jesus' Name, Amen." (Ironically, this would be the same hotel that I would stay in five months later as Nathaniel received brain surgery).

Later that day while at the hospital, the medical team came to my dad's room and said they were going to try to remove the breathing tube again. They didn't sound too hopeful, but my family was very prayerful. The medical team asked us to leave the room, and after some time, they came back to tell us that Dad was breathing on his own! Praise the Lord!

Now fast forward five months later, when things had turned drastically for the worse with Nathaniel, it was my dad who called me at 3AM on May 25th. In tears, he said, "God woke me up, and I am praying differently for Nathaniel." I knew exactly what my dad meant, and he continued, "You know what God can do because you saw what He did for me. But that may not be what God wants for Nathaniel. And we will have to accept what God allows."

Surrendering to God's sovereignty means praising God and trusting Him even when He doesn't do what I ask, the way I want Him to do it. Even though God chose not to keep Nathaniel on earth with us, He is the same good God that chose to heal my dad. Therefore, I choose to praise Him: Blessed be the name of the Lord!

Trusting God's sovereignty doesn't change the intense ache that I experience. There is such a deep-rooted void that overshadows the physical, emotional, and mental aspects of my daily life. Seeing couples at church, the grocery store, or in the car beside me at a traffic light can trigger a range of emotions. I must be intentional and deliberate with identifying my thoughts and feelings so that I don't end up getting stuck on a road of anguish, despair, and downheartedness.

Being honest and vulnerable with God has been most helpful. What a privilege to approach the throne of grace with courage and confidence that He will not leave me where I am (Hebrews 4:16). Being able to say, "Lord, I miss Nathaniel so much… Lord, I surrender this pain and emptiness. Please fill me." The Lord promises to be *near to the brokenhearted* (Psalm 34:18). *He is my refuge and strength, a very present help in trouble* (Psalm 46:1).

Insight

1) Close your eyes and visualize what "surrender" looks like for you.

2) List 5 phrases that match your visual. For example, "white flag", "let go", etc.

_____
_____
_____
_____
_____

3) Write a prayer of surrender to GOD. Ask Him to help you to recall your phrases whenever you become anxious. Tell Him your challenges, exactly what makes it difficult to surrender. Be honest by telling God exactly what is in your heart.

_____
_____
_____
_____
_____
_____
_____

Point to Ponder:

Cease striving and know that I am GOD. Psalm 46:10

In Secondary Losses

Out of everyone in the house, Nathaniel used to adjust the thermostat the most. As I returned home after making his funeral arrangements, I walked into my house and noticed that it was extremely warm. In ninety-degree weather, my indoor thermostat read eighty-one degrees. The thermostat indicated that the air conditioning was on. However, there was warm air blowing from the vents. I immediately searched the internet and called different heating and air companies to compare prices. My regular maintenance man had informed me that he could not come until the following afternoon. Another company told me that they couldn't come until the day after the next. By the evening, it had become unbearably warmer, and my two dogs were so miserable that they barely moved. We even attempted to open doors and windows, as it was cooler outside than it was inside.

I was an emotional wreck and began to cry. I was not used to being responsible to handle appliance malfunctions on my own. I knew that if Nathaniel were still with me, he would know exactly what to do or who to call to get the job done. Suddenly, I thought to check my house's circuit breaker. It had never crossed my mind that this could be the cause of our air conditioning problem. However, I never had to think of this kind of stuff before. The circuit breaker had tripped. With just one flip of a switch, we had cold air again. What a dreadful reminder that my "man-of-the-house" was no longer with me.

Yardwork

Another chore that I've never ever had to think about in the past was yardwork. As a matter of fact, before we bought our home, I asked Nathaniel if he was okay with all the anticipated landscaping. Truthfully, he seemed to be most content working outside in the yard. Now, less than three years later, Joyce and I are learning to mow the lawn, and we were doing an okay job at it. That is, until the mower stopped working, and we learned that the belt had broken. I made a call to see if I could order the needed belt, and I was asked, "Which belt do you need?" Just a simple question, but another harsh truth that *"if Nathaniel were here, I would not have to know anything about the mower and its belts!"*

Car Troubles

After midnight, Kristine came home from work and reported that her car was making "funny noises," and there were dashboard warning lights. The next morning, she decided to drive Nathaniel's old car to work since she didn't feel secure with hers. By that afternoon, my car started making a screeching, clunking noise. It got worse the more I drove it, so I decided to call for roadside assistance. Kristine came to pick me up from work in her dad's car. When we got home, the car window would not roll up. I assumed, from experience, that the power window was off track. After struggling to do what had looked easy when Nathaniel had done it before, I crumbled in frustration and defeat. On emotional overload, my sorrow was intensified by a day of car misfortunes.

Recognizing that the problem is not the air conditioner, lawn mower, nor the cars, but it is the conclusion that the death of my husband is the actuality of many losses.

Nathaniel, you have been my faithful friend and lover, sparring partner, my sense of security, my constant... no matter what, you were there. Even if you could not fix it, you were my shoulder to lean on, chest to rest upon, strong arms to hold me, and the voice that reassured me that we were okay... my constant. A major loss.

Insight

1) Think about a time that you became really upset, angry, frustrated, or overly emotional. Were your emotions misdirected?
2) How do you deal with your frustrations?
3) List healthy and safe people in whom you can confide.
4) Write a prayer asking GOD to show you the areas that have been negatively affected by your loss. How do you want Him to help you? Be honest by telling God exactly what is in your heart.

_____
_____
_____
_____
_____
_____
_____
_____
_____
_____
_____
_____
_____
_____
_____
_____
_____
_____

Point to Ponder:
Identifying the problem is the first step to healing and growth.

In My Grief

Just eleven days after Nathaniel died, I attended my first GriefShare meeting. For many, this would seem entirely too soon, but it was exactly what I needed to gently guide me through my initial pain and sorrow. GriefShare became a safety net into which I looked forward to falling weekly. It was a place where others were well-acquainted with grief, and each were in their different phases. I always knew that I would hear useful tips that I could apply while learning to grieve *unapologetically*.

One of the most valuable Scripture verses that they shared was *"Blessed are those who mourn, for they shall be comforted"* (Matt. 5:4). This verse reminded me that I must mourn in order to be comforted, giving me permission to enter my grief without reservation. If I felt like talking, I could talk, or if I felt like crying, I could do that. GriefShare also prompted me that it is okay to ask for help and the value of saying exactly what I need. Most importantly, GriefShare's daily devotions helped me to apply God's Word as a Healing Balm for my broken heart.

GriefShare prepared me for what is known as "grief ambushes," emotions that just come out of nowhere. I understand that they are to be expected, and that I can give myself time for those tears. One day, while I headed home from work, I was struck by the thought that there was no real need to rush home, because Nathaniel was not there for me to prepare his dinner. Joyce and Kristine had other plans… the house would be empty. There'd be no one to ask how my day was or how I was feeling.

Ambushed! The tears poured out uncontrollably, and I let them. I walked into my home, let the dogs outside, and was immediately crushed by the silence. I allowed myself to feel the pain, emptiness, and anguish. There's nothing like a good cleansing cry. After some time, I called my friend and asked her to pray for me. Praise God for the gift of prayerful, spirit-filled friends who are great listeners!

On my first day back to work, I went outside to put something into the mailbox. Upon my return, it dawned on me that Nathaniel will never drop by for another surprise lunch visit. Ambushed! With sobs, I collapsed into the arms of Rita, our Center Director. Thankfully, there were no clients present. God has extended His hand of love through Rita and my coworkers who are like family! These sisters-in-Christ are attentive to my emotional and spiritual needs, praying for me, and allowing me grace to heal at my own pace. However, because there are times when I cannot just let the emotional waves roll, GriefShare has encouraged me to prepare an "emotional escape plan." Since that first day back to work, I have learned to take a walk, excuse myself from a conversation, or to do whatever is necessary to redirect my focus.

Insight

Consider joining a grief support group. You will find that you are not alone. Help, hope, and healing is available.

www.griefshare.org

Point to Ponder:

"... I will turn your mourning into gladness; I will give them comfort and joy instead of sorrow." Jeremiah 31:13

In Moments of Mourning

Nathaniel had retired from his job just 11 months before his surgery. He had bucket list plans, which included home projects. One home project was an outdoor screen house. I had previously mentioned that I would like to have a screened in area in the backyard. I said it, and it was his pleasure to try to make it happen. That's my Nathaniel! His eyes always said to me, "I wish I could give you the world."

The outdoor screen house was only half complete when Nathaniel passed away. I struggled pulling into the yard looking at this unfinished project. Upon looking through his belongings, I found his project folder. It had the name, address, and quote that someone had projected for the completion of the screen house. I called the gentleman, named Mr. Frank, and explained that, since Nathaniel had died, I could not carry out all his original plans and designs, but that I would like a quote to at least have the screen house closed in.

Mr. Frank came by and gave me a new quote to which I agreed. After about a week of him working on the screen house, I walked into the backyard one day after work and was moved to tears. He had completed the task. He had done a phenomenal job above and beyond what I ever expected. With a flood of emotion, I remember thinking that Nathaniel is not here to see this. He can't ever sit in the finished product. He can't enjoy the design that he imagined. How sad!

Just as quickly as those tears rolled down my cheeks, the thought came to my mind that there's no comparison to the joys and pleasures that are in Heaven. *Nathaniel is in paradise with Jesus.* I realized that I had just experienced a moment of joy and pain, peace and mourning! For as much as I miss Nathaniel, I know that he *is* in the best place and would not want to return to this world, because he is with the Son of God.

Insight

1) Have you ever experienced joy and pain at the same time? 2) Write a prayer to GOD about a painful situation in which you would like to see/feel His peace. Be honest by telling God exactly what is in your heart.

_____
_____
_____
_____
_____
_____
_____
_____
_____
_____
_____
_____
_____
_____
_____
_____
_____
_____
_____
_____
_____

Point to Ponder:

And the *peace* of God, which *passes* all *understanding*, shall keep your hearts and minds through Christ Jesus. Philippians 4:7

In My Praise

Another time, I was at home alone… the quiet empty house. I began to cry. After a few minutes, I said, "Well, I can either cry a puddle onto this floor or I can use this time to praise God." I grabbed the anointing oil and began to invite the Lord into my home as the Head of the house, Priest, Provider, and Protector. Nathaniel, Joyce, Theo, Kristine, and I had blessed our home when we first moved in. However, under new circumstances, I chose to re-dedicate and reestablish His reign. I walked from room to room, anointing and praising God for His provision, presence, and protection. I took the oil and decided to anoint my outdoor premises. I'm pretty sure the neighbors were wondering, "What is this crazy lady pouring on the ground?"

Then, I decided to grab my cell phone and earbuds, with intentions of playing praise music and doing some quick walking for exercise while making a mental gratitude list. However, my phone rang, and it was my Aunt Dobby. I started walking and talking with her about the goodness of Jesus. Before I knew it, I was walking faster and faster and my hands went up in the air. The presence of the Lord fell upon me and I began worshiping the Lord. Eyes closed, hands up, tears streaming, and mouth filled with praise! Aunt Dobby was worshiping with me on the phone. Eventually, I joyfully exclaimed, "Aunt Dobby, I am in my front yard praising the Lord!"

I will cry. I will mourn. But I will trust God for the joy that can only come from Him. Scripture says that *weeping may endure for the night, but joy comes in the morning* (Psalm 30:5). And I believe that I will have moments of joy even in my *mourning*. The *joy of the Lord is my strength* (Nehemiah 8:10).

Insight

1) Make a gratitude list of all the things for which you are grateful including good memories.

2) Write a prayer to GOD giving Him permission to renew your joy in ways that only He can. Be honest by telling God exactly what is in your heart.

_____
_____
_____
_____
_____
_____
_____
_____
_____
_____
_____
_____
_____
_____
_____
_____
_____
_____
_____
_____
_____
_____

Point to Ponder:
There is always something for which to be thankful!

In HIS Promises

I have never experienced such unique, intimate times with the Lord. He has been my Wonderful Counselor. My prayer times have been intense because my needs are immense. I have chosen to lean into my greatest Resource, and He continues to hold me close, comforting me, and speaking His promises over my life.

I remember talking to God while driving to work one day. I had hit an "if only" moment. My mind took me back to one year prior to Nathaniel's death. He was considering retirement, and we were looking at our budget and financial obligations. Health insurance was going to become a major monthly bill. I listed our monthly bills, and it was apparent that we would be spending over half of our income on the car insurance, health insurance, life insurance, mortgage insurance, etc. It was ridiculous. I vividly remember showing him the list and saying, "We will be struggling to pay all of these insurances… we cannot afford this… either we trust God or we don't."

Through the process of elimination, the only insurance that we could realistically do away with was mortgage insurance. Legally, one has to have car and health insurance, so they were not an option. We talked and prayed about it and, within a month, decided that with the increase of health insurance premiums, we should discontinue the mortgage insurance.

The decision to keep the health insurance was the better decision. It was proven to be necessary, important, and beneficial. However, in the aftermath of death, I was in the car saying to the Lord, "God, I prayed about it... if you would have told me to keep the mortgage insurance, I would have..."

In the middle of those prayer/thoughts, God said "Nathaniel died. I did not. I am your Provider. I have always provided for you. I will provide for you."

What a profound message from the Lord, putting things back into perspective. Yes, I can feel the physical effects of my loss. However, God is still God. His promises are still "yes and amen" (2 Corinthians 1:20). He is my heavenly Father who knows what I have need of (Matthew 6:31-32).

"Either we trust God or we don't." Wow. I heard the words that I had spoken to Nathaniel coming right back.

I replied, "Lord, I will trust You. You are trustworthy."

Some months later, I was at the bank drive through window, and out of nowhere panic hit me. "What if something happens to you, your job, your health, your car? It's just you now. What if???"

We do know that fear is not from the Lord. *God has not given us a spirit of fear* (2 Timothy 1:7). If we're not careful fear becomes a slippery slope down which we can easily slide. But thank God for Jesus, His Word, and His promises.

I grasped hold to the following four words: I AM your Provider. I began to say, "Thank You, Lord" until my heart was at ease! Those times that I am afraid I will trust You (Psalm 56:3).

A day later I stopped at my mailbox, as usual, and headed into the house. In the mail I found a card from a dear friend. It was not unusual to receive special little notes from her on occasions. However, that day was a God-ordained occasion. The card had a $100 bill in it with a note that read as follows:

*... this gift is from God. He just
reminded me that He is on this gift.
It says IN GOD WE TRUST. So, I
think He's telling you that we can
trust Him...*

Nobody but God knew of the moment that I had recently experienced at the bank. He chose to demonstrate His promise through an unexpected card and a $100 bill that reminded me in God I trust!

Insight

1) Write a prayer to GOD praising Him for who He is. If it is difficult to write from your heart, write Scripture passages about the character of GOD. Be honest by telling God exactly what is in your heart.

_____
_____
_____
_____
_____
_____
_____
_____
_____
_____
_____
_____
_____
_____
_____
_____
_____
_____
_____

Point to Ponder:
If you want to keep GOD close, praise Him! God dwells in the praise of His people. (Psalm 22:3)

In HIS perfect timing

Lastly, I thank God for His timing. I will never know it all, nor do I have to. *The secret things belong to the LORD our God* (Deuteronomy 29:29a). In my limited thinking, I cannot always see the perfection of God's timing. But I know that I serve an all-knowing, wise God that never makes a mistake.

I do recognize that if Nathaniel had died 10 years ago when he had surgery for the first pituitary adenoma, I would have been left to raise three teenagers by myself. Everything would have been so different. I am thankful for the years that I was blessed to have Nathaniel in my life. Thank You, Lord, for the children that were birthed and nurtured from our union: My children were able to reach adulthood with the assistance of both parents. Thank God that I have experienced true love--- the ups, downs, twists-and-turns kind of love!

Today, I am in a more mature place in every aspect of my life--- physically, emotionally, financially, and especially, spiritually. God has used all our past, all of the things that He has brought us through, to remind me of His faithfulness. *This I recall to my mind, therefore have I hope. It is of the Lord's mercies that we are not consumed, because His compassions fail not. They are new every morning: great is Thy faithfulness. The Lord is my portion, saith my soul; therefore, will I hope in Him* (Lamentations 3: 21-26 KJV).

My hope is in the Lord. Through my tears, questions, and fears, I will praise Him. Lord, please help me to continually trust Your heart and to choose to see Your hand.

When all is said and done, I know that the safest place in this whole wide world is in **HIS** hands.

In conclusion, (not because God is finished), I am learning that praying and trusting in God will not always mean that I get the results I want in the way I want them. Sincere prayer helps me to surrender my will to His, trusting that His plan is always greater than mine. And even when I don't understand His plan, I can know and believe that His thoughts are always good toward me (Jeremiah 29:11). Therefore, I can seek Him wholeheartedly, making a conscious choice to see Him, to see His hand, and to trust Him through it all (Jeremiah 29:13). There, I find my purpose, our purpose: To worship and praise our God.

I will bless the LORD at all times and HIS praise will continually be in my mouth (Psalm 34:1).

Insight

1) Make a declaration of your decision to choose to see GOD in the midst of adversity and trouble. Will you praise Him, trust Him, and surrender to His will? Let your own words form a covenant between you and GOD.

<u>Lord, today I realize that I may not always get what I want the way that I want it. But that doesn't mean that You don't love me. You are always for me, pursuing me, drawing me to Yourself. Even when I can't see You or feel You, help</u>

<u>me to remember that You are with me. In difficult times, please help me to remember, and adhere to, my following declarations. Yes, I will… (Fill in the blanks with your own person declarations to God… Be honest with your intent).</u>

_____
_____
_____
_____
_____
_____
_____
_____
_____
_____
_____
_____
_____
_____

Celebrating God's Faithfulness

Through the years!

www.ingramcontent.com/pod-product-compliance
Lightning Source LLC
Chambersburg PA
CBHW052126110526
44592CB00013B/1766